C000053086

The Mayapple Forest

The Mayapple Forest

Kim Ports Parsons

Terrapin Books

© 2022 by Kim Ports Parsons
Printed in the United States of America.
All rights reserved.
No part of this book may be reproduced in any manner,
except for brief quotations embodied in critical articles
or reviews.

Terrapin Books
4 Midvale Avenue
West Caldwell, NJ 07006

www.terrapinbooks.com

ISBN: 978-1-947896-59-8
Library of Congress Control Number: 2022942401

First Edition

Cover art: Frances Coates
Mayapples
Acrylic on canvas "25-3/4" x "37-3/4"

Cover Design: Diane Lockward

In memory of my mother, Ouida Jenette Ports

Contents

To pray you open your whole self
To sky, to earth, to sun, to moon
To one whole voice that is you.
　　　　　　—Joy Harjo, "Eagle Poem"

One

This Kind of Rainfall

Rain after rain, sun after rain,
the mountain throws its scarf of mist

across the valley. Rivulets form, disperse,
re-form, disperse again. Bittersweet

quietly takes over the hedgerow.
You there?   *You there?*

A bobwhite gently repeats his question.
They say this kind of rainfall,

day after day, inch after inch, comes once
in a hundred years. On the garden fence,

cucumbers demonstrate the declarative,
gold trumpets blaring. Determination,

my mother taught me. The way rock
is sanded down by water, the hoe's handle

worn smooth. Keep going.
Hat, boots, and gloves wait by the door.

Clouds line up at the exit.
I'm here.   *I'm here.*

The constant, silent ticking
of her absence.

Time to Carry

I can't recall the date, can only guess the hour,
but it's time to get up and walk the dog
and put the seed out for the birds
whose feathers know it's time to fade and hide
among the undressing hedges.

I'm not sure whether it's Monday or Tuesday
or Sunday, but it's cool this morning, time to move
sweaters up on the shelves, time to find the other glove
before we sink our feet into the frosty dew
and sniff the sunrise, later each morning,

more orange, lower on the horizon, as day ascends.
It's time to walk, then to sip coffee, then
read the news, then despair again, of emperors
and their antics, push through and begin
the morning's work: clearing dead vines,

deadheading the fading metaphors.
The gifts of these months of plague and separation
are silence and space and time, not calendars,
not plots on a line, but to be alive,
to breathe, to wake, to hear the owl's call,

the coyotes as they hunt and cry,
to look up and see the heron pass,
to look down and feel the cat brush my leg.
I imagine children climbing trees.
I mow the grass when it grows long.

Then it's time to scrub the floor on bended knees.
Time to cook the sauce. The fruit is ripe.
Now it's time to wake, now time to sleep.
Take this pail of water to the field,
the wooden handle cutting deep,

the millions more sickening,
millions dead, number on the grinding
wheel. I do not know the time.
This is the plague's gift: to live, to breathe,
to carry this grief, the slowing of each step.

First Paper

The kitchen down to its bones.
Fridge gone, sink gone. No faux brick
above the double oven. No oven.
No arguments at the dinner table.
No table. No mother stirring the soup.
All five layers of linoleum, scratched
by high chairs, stained by Jell-O,
scuffed by school shoes, lifted.
The book of our decades withdrawn.

The new owner's sent pictures.
Blue paneling removed. Red, white, and blue
wallpaper torn away. Stubborn scraps
patterned like a child's loud pajamas.
My father's calculations on scarred plaster,
time capsule in carpenter's pencil.
He wasn't angry that day, though surely
we were under foot, no help at all.
He whistled in splattered trousers,
his strong left hand flourished the wall.

How is it possible I remember?
Mesmerized as my sister traced and sounded
out the words and grinned under his rare praise.
It was all hieroglyphics to me, lines
and shapes vibrating with the unknown.

He printed his signature Polytechnic style,
in square and leaning capitals,
our names, formal and proud,
the date, and a declaration,

MY DAUGHTERS HELPED REMOVE OLD PAPER
as if to say to some admiring future world,
BEHOLD. WE WERE HERE. WE MADE THIS.

Book me a passage. Steer past this
aging surface, unadorned and listing south,
past the adoring wife, the lonely shoals,
the siren, the supplicant, all that pasting
and painting and putty-knifing of the self.
Keep going, all the way back to that face looking up,
reaching for the pencil to make my own marks.

Fixing Thelma's Hair

Her hair thin enough to show her gray-white scalp,
the skin of her neck soft as a young girl's.
She holds the bag of plastic curlers in her lap.
I stand behind the chair and comb out
the tangles from her kitchen sink shampoo.
Her toes pump up and down like pistons.

We're alone in a breeze ruffling the window
by the fridge. I begin the first row from forehead
to crown, each curler rolled toward me and held down
tight, snapped into place with green plastic.
The neat lines, the damp hair pulled straight between
my fingers, the rhythm and order, they comfort me.

The blur of her constant talk is a radio
left on for company. I interrupt to tease
about all her boyfriends, how she's been stepping
out to paint the town, dancing in her red dress.
She giggles, then sighs. *Oh, honey, I can't hardly*
even walk my hip's getting so bad. Passes me

another curler over her shoulder. When the last
one's in place, we sit at the table and sip
iced tea and try the bourbon balls she's made,
little cookies like a shot of whiskey.
I like the intimacy of a woman
in curlers, swollen feet in old, cracked mules,

tapping the tiles. She tells me the story,
the prickly halo of her head nodding, how she dared
to get a bob in the summer of 1921
on a visit to Aunt Minnie in Arlington,
how she cut off all her fine, long, white-blonde hair,
and when she got home to Shamrock, Texas,

her mother vowed never to speak to her sister again,
and Grandaddy Riley went out to the shed to get drunk.
Pretty soon, all six of her sisters followed suit. She's a tough one,
energy springing from her like the tight curls off the rollers
as I comb her out. Before I shape the hair and spray its familiar
pattern, I run my fingers through the Miss Clairol gold

and feel the fragile bowl of her skull.
It won't be long before she lays it down.

Why I Couldn't Stay
in the Midwest Any Longer

Eight years in the center of the endless plains,
wading through snow drifts in October, plodding
into a north wind, ice on my eyelashes,
waiting and waiting and waiting for a spring
that lasted one week, then fanning myself
in front of a rickety window unit in a rented flat,
watching hail the size of gumballs ping off windshields,
walking wide, planned streets, Eastern trees placed
to shade boulevards and American Craftsman houses
but with leaves that never quite changed color, just dropped
to the sidewalk, worn out and blanched by September.

I missed Baltimore, its familiar, cramped corners,
Little Italy, the delis, Germantown,
Greektown, the muddy Patapsco, the putrid water
of the harbor, the smell of McCormick spice,
so I dragged my sorry muffler across 1200
miles, one elbow out the window,
burning in the June sun, and almost stopped the car
to kiss the ground when I hit familiar rolling hills,
an old backroad we cruised, FM radio blaring,
woozy from Boone's Farm and too much flirtation.
Never could get used to being too far from big water,

the choppy, briny bay, gulls on the cobblestones,
diners and spicy seafood, and it didn't feel right,
everyone looking alike, chronically polite,
no one ever suddenly chatting you up
about their mom's best crab soup recipe
while picking out produce at the IGA,
just sitcom faces. I guess that's a bit harsh,
and folks were so nice, but I felt loud with strangers
there, among the subdued, longed to whoop and holler
and jump up to dance like hallelujah
when a band kicked on at a Friday Fells Point bar.

But the real reason I couldn't stay
was my jigsaw puzzle heart, fallen,
slipped out the side of an old wooden crate,
unnoticed, side-split, scattered down the curb.
I figured if I went where my feet fit
the contours of the ground, then maybe I
could sort the pieces under the glow
of the Domino sugar sign down by the water,
find my shape again in the eyes of friends.
They'd buy me a drink and not mind my crying
into it, until I didn't need to anymore.

I Want to Ride Through This Life

—for Doug

like a child standing on the hump
of an old sedan, leaning over
the front bench seat,
not knowing what's beyond
but full of eager anticipation,
gleaming windshield of possibility,
sun breaking through greening trees.
You drive, beloved.
I know you'll go gently,
assuring it's not too far
or too long or too hard,
that wonderful things are waiting.
Along the way, songs we know
and sing along, and new songs,
and special things to eat and drink,
and games with words, and laughter.
And space for silence, too,
for sleeping, and even dreams.
You'll go just fast enough
on a country lane, mountains
in the blue distance, that
if I jump as we climb a cresting hill,
and if I catch the moment just right,
my jump will become
w e i g h t l e s s n e s s—

a suspension, a floating in joy,
a kind of flying,
a hawk testing its wings
on its first miraculous glide.

A Lesson in Joy

—for Sandy Yannone

Most days the news presses me further into the reckoning
of the dead horse we are beating, you know the one,
the drumming hoofbeats of our imminent demise. Not the earth's,
no—whatever we leave or lose or toss aside or pile up,
she will cover, grow over, wear down, grind down,
transform to soil, or bury under tar.
       Twenty-five years ago,
I bumped into my friend in the hallway of the building
where we taught, on a Friday afternoon, and I told her
I was ready to cash it in and just go get lost somewhere,
let go of time and appointments. She looked at her watch,
unbuckled the band, and gracefully, confidently, skipped it down
the tiled floor like a boy skillfully flicking a stone along
the skin of a perfectly smooth pond.
       She grinned at me,
threw her head back and laughed, then I laughed too,
and it was like the long, giddy, glide down a very steep
hill, on a wide open country road, after a hard pull on the pedals.
Bless her and that tossed watch, how it has skimmed the surface
on murky days, broken the skin of despair or grief with its joy,
how the child in me has floated up, the child spirit
who wants to live, to pick up a pebble, to carry it home
to my writing desk, to ripple her laughter back.

Barn Owl

She has a heart-shaped face, buff white feathers,
dark eyes, hunts in open country, along wooded edges,
makes her home in hollow trees, ghost-like,
sees creatures moving in the meadow while we're sleeping.

Most think sight her strength, and it's true—she can find
a whisker in a haystack—but her hearing is so sharp,
so especially keen, in fact, that if the window's left open
when the moon is full, and the frogs finish their chorus,

and the air is still and cool as a fresh sheet,
then perhaps, as she glides on tawny wings
simply because she can, free and satisfied, not yet
brooding a second clutch, she lands and preens

on the rooftop, daylight still an hour away,
turns her neck in the hush and hears,
without the slightest interest, the murmured notes
we offer, stirring in our nest.

Two

The Daily Subtraction of Grief

Turn my back to the sun to bring the scissors into focus,
then cut five peonies and one bud from the lowest branches
of the same plant which grew in the backyard
for forty-seven years, before that who knows how
many decades by Aunt Minnie's front porch.
Make the cuts about ten inches down the stem
to fill the old vase which sat on Grandmother's console
beside her collection of six brass bells.

Don't try to count the petals. Soft white surrounding
finite pink centers, marked with three bright stigmas
like a trinity of Mama's red lipsticks.
So many more flowers were transposed
from the homeplace, but today, just pick these.
It's impossible to calculate how long their presence
will carry me over, or the number of times
I will bring my face down to the peonies,
to solve for a fragrance equal to the missing total
of my mother's ceaseless heart.

Hope is the thing with feathers

The starling jumps down into the hole,
bits of brown clutched in her yellow beak.
The cheeping from below is an echo
of yearning. Once a summer storm yanked

this trunk in two. Hidden in the tangled
growth, a wound becomes a refuge.
The gutters this side of the roof, so long
neglected, sprout seedlings which lean into

the white rail and wave, ladies at a balustrade,
happy passengers about to embark
on a doomed ship. This balcony floats,
tethered among the branches. Billowing

sails of leaf-printed silk, inhale and exhale,
sunlight over shadow. No one loves
a starling, yet she weathers the swales.
Such a bird, each spring, commandeers the heart.

She prepares a nest and ties it fast, wants
to set sail, to fling caution to the wind.
She perches on the mast, and with rusty
clicks and old tin whistles, she starts to sing.

Summer Storms

I

In the slow heat of the July afternoon, the laundry
crowded the back yard in thick lines, the sheets
hanging limply between the tall oaks, the heavy air

filling them slowly, then falling away. Before
the thunder and lightning and black clouds took
the hill, where our house waited, exposed, looking out

over Leonard's acres of corn, I stood, still,
behind the garden in the grassy field of wild
strawberry, and watched the sheets of water dragging

slowly back and forth across the furrows a half mile away.
I watched them come closer to the house, over the silver
queen stretching away to the woods, above the horse corn

in all its dry, hard fullness, and in the light turning
deep yellow and brown under water, my mother came out
with the first flashes, the back door slamming shut

behind her, her hair blown back, her arms strong around
the basket, her mouth open, a dark line, her words past
me, so quick I ran to the lines, and together we loaded

the basket, our arms, rushed in, back up the steps,
heard the first lamp crash to the floor in the front room,
raced to shut all the windows against the water rising

in the sills, the wind filling up the rooms, the branches
snapping, the dark light gathering in the kitchen, in the
piles of damp clothes on the table, the rain spitting off the cement,

the cool, green rush through the wet screen door.

II
All summer, the cows came wandering into our yard
from Ward's farm, over the hill, and they stood,

chewing cud under the oaks like it was home,
until Ward's shy son came to fetch them. And then,

in August, our old beagle, Scout, left his cries
for the rabbits in the fields, and died, asleep

in a mud puddle under the truck. At dusk, when the cool
thunder washed over the house, we all kneeled

on the couch and watched through the picture window,
huddled together like the cows against the coming storm.

During the night, lightning split an old straight
hickory, travelled through the ground, hit the house,

came clear into my bedroom, shattering the lamp hanging
over my bed, and I woke up, sitting in shards, uncut.

Out in the living room, Uncle Bob's cigarette flashed
yellow, then red, as we all sat together, whispering,

waiting for it to end. In the morning, the tree still
stood, striped all the way to the ground with the line

of fire, and deep ruts in the lawn felt their way
to the house like muddy fingers. Even so, in the bright

sun, the hot tar on the road popped under my bare feet,
and the cows gathered like shadows under the willow.

This Is Not a Sestina about Quarks

Though it may have a similar flavor,
this is not a sestina about quarks.
Repeat *up—down—charm—strange—top—bottom—*
and anything might fit. For example,
one afternoon, a man walks to the home
of the woman he left for another.

She's planting four o'clocks in the garden
when she feels his eyes on her back, jerks up,
twists her neck to look, pushes her spade down
into the soil like a protective charm.
A sudden weight, ghost hand pressing the top
of her chest, and her stomach bottoms out.

He comes into focus, there, in shadow,
the alley across the street, sizing up
whether or not to approach. From the top
floor, Mozart comes drifting. Should he go back
downtown? back to his new place with its strange
flavor of regret? Starting over has its charms.

She stands, steadies herself, the top
spin of betrayal, a strong force down.
She focuses on the landscape of his face,
the sad line of mouth, the quirky charm
of the scar biting the bottom lip so
often kissed. Better to shift the eyes up,

make a viewfinder, forefingers and thumbs
combining in a makeshift frame, panning
to sky, to hawk circling over rooftops.
Rules are sometimes broken, lovers estranged.
Better still, a microscope. Look down
on the atomic emptiness stirring

at the bottom of everything. Or up
so far there is no "up," past the cloud
of cosmic debris strangely orbiting.
At the known world's bottom, quarks are spinning.
It's all spinning, I reckon, clear to the top.
Four o'clocks bloom in the late sun's charm.

There's no safe path down to the bottom. She shakes her head.
He becomes a stranger then, gives up, and turns away.
She learns to spin her heart like a top. It works like a charm.

A Blessing

You sit on your front porch some evening,
alone, or holding the hand of someone you love,
or not holding it, nor your breath, nor your stiff
neck of work. Your mind slowly opens
with the drifting down of dusk.

Little twitches of the calendar pass through
your arms and legs. Let them. They can't dance
you back into dailiness. Even the flashes
of pain once inflicted you brush off
as you do the mosquitoes. (These steal small portions

of your blood—don't give them more.)
And while you wander over yourself and settle
into the shadows, the moonflower on the vine
twining up the porch rail slowly opens, so slowly
you don't turn your head.

                              You do not drag
the heavy tail of him behind you anymore.
You have lifted him in your arms and turned him over
and known his human shape once again.
When you set him down, he walked away.

Turn now. Feel some presence at your back.
See the full circle of the blossom.
And though momentary, how it glows,
how its purity washes over you,
its scent a sacred, open space.

Life Goals

To see, the way a coneflower sees
a carpenter bee, vibrating with hunger
and need. To need, the way a stone requires
rain, wind, time, and gravity's pull.
To pull, the way a birch pulls from its core
without practice or instruction, bends to
grass with grace, forgiving the wind's trespasses.
To forgive and hold firm, as the goldfinch
on the thin, swaying stalk of millet in March.
To shine as this same finch when summer comes,
flashing sun on broken glass, loop of golden air.
To hear, the way the mole hears, through every hair,
the next shining moment of the underground day,
a lighthouse made of sound, life at the root.

Love, Birds

Despite their best efforts,
a pair of young bluebirds

aren't succeeding with their first nest.
They've chosen a house you built

for others: a kind of lean-to for robins, phoebes,
and song sparrows. Only three sides,

an open floor, a slanting roof, a space exposed,
so each beginning is easily dismissed by wind.

My early love affairs were like that,
but Oh, that swoon of blue—

She gathers dry grasses.
He stands guard on the barbecue.

Hers is a cup of hope, possibility, so fragile.
It never fails to make me smile

when a male cardinal at the feeder
delivers a seed to a female

with what appears to be a kiss.
So I should greet you, each day.

What good does it do to chastise ourselves,
as years pass, for our lack of bright feathers?

Perhaps my memory fails me, but wasn't it a barred owl
we heard that first weekend we spent making love?

I recall starting a poem, a love note really,
about calling out for my heart's desire.

Each night, this June, we hear the whippoorwill,
insistent, tireless, randy. Sometimes he is so loud

we have to close the windows to sleep.
When we wake, I curve my body

in gratitude, and feather my fingers through yours.
I suggest that perhaps you could attach

a small addition to the platform, like an arm
to hold the nest. It would be easy to cut

a piece of scrap and tack it on. Sure, you say,
and go out to your wood shop, and get to work.

Mayapple Jelly

Despite the name, there's no fruit in May; it ripens, mellow
and rare, under July's ragged umbrella. You need two cups, pectin,
sugar, and lemon. Stir the honey-guava, simmering yellow.
Strain away the poison of the pulp, seeds, and skin.

Taste the singular fruit, sweet and sour, thickened by pectin.
Consider its names—racoon berry, ground apple, wild mandrake.
Strain life's poisons. It's finished when you skim
a spoon and two distinct drops run together, sheeting from a plate.

Consider ways to name the pain. Heart's mandrake?
Label and shelve. Some days, small spoonfuls are cathartic.
When a life drops, edges scrape like tectonic plates.
Mayapple roots grow underground in winter, their poison cytostatic.

(Meaning cells that won't divide.) Shelve your losses. Taste spoonfuls
in remembrance. Wait for the sweetness, memory's calf.
Mothers may teach daughters how to smooth edges, how to placate
pain, how to keen a song of naming, how loss ripens the self.

Three

Golden Purslane

The seed packet promises *fifty days*
of golden-hued leaves among the greens,
larger and more upright in its ways

than its wild cousin, gangly and fey,
which seeds itself, stretching grayish green.
The seed packet promises fifty days

crisp and brightly flavored, swallowtails
who pause, drift away, beetles who scurry unseen
beneath the large, upright, golden displays,

leaving spirograph designs in the loam, arrays
of hidden lives, promises of rolling in the clover, green
and lush, of salads, soups, whole picnics for days,

stir fries, stews, wine and cheese, fragrant bouquets.
Dragonflies will land, hover and sway, bright green
and larger still, upright, glinting in their way.

Fresh furrows mark a passage on the page.
To plant a seed is to know exactly what I mean:
to plant a promise, a golden packet of days,
to grow larger and more upright in your ways.

I Watch My Sister Harvest Lavender

—for Terry

She sits at the edge of the porch,
curved over the plants, her bare feet
on the cool grass, the hot sun shining
on her shoulders, the curling brown
of her hair, her cheekbones finely angled
as a deer's. She stops to sip her coffee,
her garden spreading around her,
the daylilies raising their skirts to the sky.

Suddenly, I see her as if I were again six
and she seventeen, that kind of hero worship.
I watch her through the white hot blanket of light,
a camera's flash, and all the images of the past
transposed, pentimento. The lavender is thick
with bees. She gathers a few stems in her left hand,
snips with her right. The bees circle the blossoms,
rise and fall all around her, the gray boards

of the hot porch beneath me, a watery wind in the trees.
She scatters the stems in her large brown basket
and takes another sip of coffee. She turns
to me and laughs, tells me she's lucky.
I think: You taught me how to swim.
You walked with me across a snow-crusted field.
Your body swayed before me, shaping into a woman's.
You cupped a wildflower in your palm and gave me its name.

She turns back to her task, this morning's prayer.
And her hands move through the purple-blue,
the yellow-black. She explains how she leaves some,
in part for the bees, in part for herself,
until new buds grow, and fill out with flowers once more.
She leans into the light. The light leads me
to her hands. And her hands teach me how to harvest
despite the danger, the necessary chance, of a sting.

The Taste of Copper

—for Jackie Ross, who gave me the first line

Pain is a penny, easily spent.
And yet, my pockets drag
with the weight I can't cast off.
I could buy you a chocolate

to roll along your tongue,
its sweetness a reminder
of your power to disdain.
I could exchange a fist

of pennies for a paper kite
to flash its bold colors
over the broken record of my thoughts.
Or here, a penny to let fall,

casually, left behind like a dream
for some child to find.
Or perhaps just this one
will buy a wish, when dropped,

hooking it like a bluegill
in the murky water of a pond.
Perhaps it will not jump
my tremulous line.

I have learned to swallow
the shiny pennies of tears,
the bitter taste of copper.
Soon, I'll drop my bags of coin

like twin anchors,
far out in the harbor of sleep,
till the fog rolls over
and the foghorn moans,

and I grow invisible—
lost to the ship
slipping dangerously close,
carrying you away.

Mermaid Summer

I found it cleaning out the cedar chest,
twelve inches of ponytail held by a pink
band, thick and sinuous, streaked white
and gold with chlorine and sun.
Water my element that summer.
While Mama read and Dad fished,
and my sister sneaked kisses behind
the dunes, I just avoided land.

I held my breath, looked up through ripples
to sky, practiced dolphin arcs, slowly released
each pearl of air, floated my compact
body with arms outstretched, at home
inside my skin. I learned to jump
incoming waves, bobbed among swells,
let human voices wash away, listened
for songs from underwater caves.

When I clambered out, savoring the pull
of my hair streaming down my back,
I walked to the showers, reveled in the soft
rain, pretended my long tail stretched sleek
and strong and glinted blue and green. How deep
could I dive? How far could I swim? How long
could I stay under, uncontained and glimmering?

Next year, my breasts began to bud. By ten, my blood
began to run. I learned new meanings of the word shame.
I told my mother I wanted my hair cut off.
I didn't know she tucked it away.

Now, some nights when I can't sleep,
my mind spins like the churning inside a wave.
I conjure myself a secret cave, on a high cliff.
I can see the empty beach for miles.
I enter and step down stone stairs to a pool, warm
and dark, and as water laps the walls and bubbles
rise from a spring far below, I steep, and then I stretch
and become myself again, and flex my shimmering tail.

Upstream

My father died suddenly,
my mother left to mourn.
Three hundred miles from home,
he turned down his bed.
Friends came for coffee,
found him on the floor.
They let my uncle know,
then we knocked on her door.

I hope his mind was on the river
where he fished the evening hatch,
steps from the old trailer
under tall pitch pines.
The water so clear there
he could count the stones.
The bourbon brown and sweet there
after casting in the dusk.

I hope the river's murmur
was louder than the pounding.
A quick death's a blessing
for the one who dies.
He washed up from supper,
then pulled back the covers,
then a sharp pain, a dizzy moment,
a door closing, and lights out.

But a curse for the one
who waits for the long box
and lays it in the ground,
who opens the window
of each empty day, and sets
a table for one each night,
who chews mouthfuls of dust,
and listens on repeat
to her own lungs' dirge.

Joy is short, the "O" a fish
makes as it leaps for the fly,
the last minute of the fifty-six
and a half years of loving a living man.
But grief, grief is long,
a strong current from which you never
rise, but needs must swim against
for the rest of your days.

Concerning Stars

Visualize a star in your heart made of blue light,
the therapist says. Not the gold stars stamped
across the stapled graphs of my childhood.
Not the bright yellow stars that I drew
above the green hill and red house.

I imagine one more like a stargazer lily,
the way it might open slowly and linger
in air, as whispers between lovers
some early morning. Or maybe it compares
to the spare stars of winter, elegant pinpoints,

a slow waltz of soldiers and ladies above snow.
In summer, stars are swimming in cream,
smeared across blue velvet and blurry
as hopscotch chalk after a long day of play.
They kept me up as a child, awake

for hide and seek, swinging through the yard.
I didn't know then about stars being born,
or dying, imploding, going supernova,
or falling into categories like tubes
of paint: giant red, blue dwarf, double yellow.

Stars were friends then, guardians, someone to hear
my confessions. Sometimes hands shine like stars
against glass, waving hello, farewell,

a code of transition: you are leaving,
I am staying, take me with you, this is goodbye.

Breathe into the star and make it grow brighter.
It glows like the signal we've come to an end.
In the universe of Hollywood,
a star like Audrey Hepburn waves to a star
like Fred Astaire, and I cry too, strings tugging

my puppet tears, stardust softening her face,
cheeks glistening like the star on Glenda's wand
drawing circles around the scene. A pretty joke
don't you see, to mistake the reflection
in someone's eyes for something else,

an entire galaxy of love, true
as the speed of light, when it's only
a dropperful of atoms bouncing back,
no more meaning than sunshine
on an apple. There is no echo

of some farther star, lodged like mine
in such dark matter. No, my cookie cutter.
You must be the bright and shining horse
I hitch my broken wagon to. Yes, my starfish,
star of wonder and wish-I-might, you'll have to do.

Cicatrice

The odd configuration caught my eye
as I knelt and weeded the fence line.
A Chinese mantis was clasping a small body,
head and throat already consumed.

Summer lunch in the garden after silent prayer,
triangular head down, metronome of the mandibles,
a bucolic horror. The entrée, ruby-throated hummingbird.
I couldn't tell if the bird were male or female.

Her throat would have been milky white, for hiding
among leaf shadows, or if his, shimmering red
for flashing, dancing arcs of display.
Cardinal vines exploded across that section

of fence, chorus of trumpets praising the sun,
and the hunter was well hid.
I planted those vines to attract and feed the hummers,
but now see what I had wrought.

Put on bright colors, decorate with blossoms,
look over the shoulder with raised eyes
and ask the ancient question. Hope the desired
will approach, partake, return, return again, and stay.

I hoped to be delicious, sustaining as manna,
a promised land. If the answer was yes,
then we each would take a long deep drink.
Sometimes you dine, sometimes you offer the dish.

The female mantis goes so far as to eat the head of her mate.
Filet the self, crack open the carapace and reveal
the earnest, insistent, wriggling mess—moles, scars,
wet mouth of want, teeming dreams of love so long sought.

That day in the garden, I inched closer,
and she raised her head, skewered me
with compound eyes, then deftly stilled herself
on the tender vine, holding tight to the uneaten half.

I stood there, transfixed by reality's pin.
Now I look down into the December garden,
the beds all cleaned and the fences bare,
an egg sac clinging to a dogwood branch.

A familiar pain comes back, just here,
under skin and bone, the old ache below flesh
once so hungrily consumed, echo of a long-healed wound,
a cicatrice, the ghost of the girl I used to be.

Four

The Poetry of Pie

The recipe card is brown and yellow and blurred,
touchstone, fingered over and over, smeary conversations
with the memorized words, written when I was still practicing
how to form an *a* or an *o*, to loop or not still undecided,
across lined paper. A bowl of peaches, warm as wool blankets
from the July air, newspaper spread under the tin bowl,
Coriolis of thumb and knife against skin, the peels collapsed
in a pile, juice crying down my arm, the slices repeating
the sunrise. The old cutter works the crumbs, ice clinks
against the tablespoon, the pastry comes together.

From the Kitchen of Jenette, I dutifully inscribed,
sitting next to her at the brown Formica table, her elbows
floury, fruity splatters on her apron's front, showing me,
when the peach is truly ripe, the skin will pull completely
away in sheets, revealing the perfect yellow glistening joy
of the flesh. Sugar, but not too much, cinnamon and nutmeg
generously sprinkled, a pinch of salt, tapioca granules like snow,
the maceration in minutes, the swoon-worthy smell.
The shuttlecock of the pin as it rolls back and forth,
back and forth, center to edge, this way, that,

till there is more than enough to meet the needs of the pan,
the crockery one with the chipped rim, then the dough
gently knuckled into the base, trimmed, fluted, filled to a mound.
Always, I forget, then drop dabs of butter with crusty hands,
weave the top, hiding the strays under the protective arms
of the lattice. She only perspired on the left side of her face,

and used her apron's hem to dab her brow, not to get flour
in her hair, to keep going, the baking, the washing up,
the fraying hot pads on the vinyl, the white cabinets
wiped down, a car pulling in the driveway,

sliced tomatoes marching down an oval platter, clothes
brought in from the line. Just a summer day, the evening cooling,
likely bad news on the TV, likely storms tomorrow, likely sisters
in a squabble, combing out knots to canned laughter after dark.
But silence settles on the room when the slices are served, as peaches,
spices, and crust intoxicate our tongues, and we all look down and chew,
and lift our forks again, and lick our lips, until finally someone says,
Why is everyone so quiet? When I sit tonight on my back porch
and share the day's pie with my husband, I will tell him this.
We will take in each bite like a tender gift. We will miss her.

Morning Practice

As the cat's bones stretch past all possibility,
as the mockingbird sings a new lexicon,
as the day's mouth opens wide,
unlock the body, turn, instinctual,
into the curve of beloved.

Rise and open the door.
Place a shallow dish of water
for the summer birds.
Choose a peach from the bowl,
cool, smooth stone on warm palm.

Place a slice on the tongue.
Sunlight in the mouth.
No need to bury that dream.
Spade a small hole in the compost pile
and drop it in. Stir.

Please Forgive Me

Please forgive me, but sometimes I talk
to the worms as I garden. I say,
Excuse me and *I'm so sorry*.
Rain calls them to the surface.

I say, *Watch out*, opening a new hole
for a pepper plant, and *There you go,
my friend*, as I cup one in my glove
and set it under the clinging peas.

The soil is soft and rich with compost.
Forgive me for what I do, I say,
for all the living sliced in two,
tunnels collapsed, barriers laid,

marches forced from a homeland.
Dust of the microbiome blooms on my skin.
Findings only prove what my instincts
already know. Such beings do a raft of good,

balance out the haves and have-nots,
create justice in the gut of us,
pursue our happiness to the very bone.
The bluebirds carry a moth to their box

and raucous celebration occurs.
Everything eats something.
If I were to gather only windfall,
or give all that I grow, or

turn the soil till my hands were torn,
I would never work as hard as they,
or give as much, or make life
from refuse, or transform the earth.

I can only speak for myself. I take,
I eat, and I kill, like all my kind.
Forgive me, but it's true, no matter how I try.
I walk with hard steps upon this only world.

Cool Glass of Water

A blizzard of fuchsia speckles all down my shirt and Mama's apron,
rivulets of sweat down the left side of her face, and my legs stuck
to the cracked vinyl seat, the kitchen getting hotter by the minute,
but we're grinning like damned fools over eight pint jars of wineberry jam,
made from the berries we picked together while ticks and poison ivy
inched up our trousers, and we sang she's coming round the mountain
and who knows what all at the top of our lungs, hoping to scare away
the snakes. I am ten, and I am spading up the last gobs from the kettle
with the wooden spoon, and I am in love with her, and if I could,
I would drink that memory like a cool glass of water every day of my life.

Death in Spring

Think of the March earth as the body's letting go.
Think of the ice melting as the last, slow breath.
Unclench. The incessant grip of winter releases
months like years, years like dark wells.
The jaw slackens, the spine slumps. The wind and rain,
their moan and slash, are death throes.
It's impossible to hold back the bright cardinals
of memory gathering in the dogwood.
The painful crust softens, and all that's frozen
morphs into a muddy dream, a vernal pool of grace.
A vase of daffodils will sit on April's table.
Grasp the lowest branch, pull, then climb
into the green and yellow sky. Blossoms,
like shy children, will turn their faces to you.

Angling

A long hike to a smooth pool below
the falls, formed in a curve of the creek,
almost still, scattered with shadows,
a spot my father might have chosen
for its mossy coolness, his hat tilted
back, sunglasses focused, waders planted
like tree trunks on the rocky bank.

A flash of yellow sky strikes the water.
How to reconcile one side of the man
with the other, all the days he was
wound so much tighter, when the evening
news sent him reeling, the protests,
the causes he could not fathom,
how he would bluster, how he wanted

to take the world by the skin of the neck
and drag it back inside his defenses.
Everyone skulked away, but not me.
I stood there and faced him, indignant,
flinging up stubborn words, both of us
tied in self-righteous knots, red-faced,
and all the arguments lost, pointless.

Above this dark pool, fists of mayfly
circle the air, and fish break the water.
Years swept the house until it was quiet.
In the den in the basement, he sat

under an angled circle of lamplight,
and thread by thread, feather by feather,
he wrapped and tied creatures of wonder,

a gnat, a nymph, a caddis, a deceiver,
mastered an art of nuance, a sport
of meditation, walked into afternoons
lightly gripping bamboo, peered through wavy
reflections, cast his line, a willow wand
skimming out and back, out and back,
then deftly, exactly, dropped, just so.

To catch a fine brook trout, to feel its strength,
reel it in, admire the sleek, speckled
skin, then oh-so-gently pull the hook
from its lip, cradle it with both hands
in the cold water just long enough
to palm its heft, ponder the length, and then,
release it, this was his practice.

If he were here with me now, he would point
out the small fish streaking through the pool,
how it stirs up the silt on the bottom,
and when that settles, the fish is gone.
He might say *you can catch one, but not really.*
You can love what you do but not yourself.
You can hold on tight, but better to just let go.

Ella: Two Ways

I

Mama takes me to hear her sing when I'm eighteen,
Ella's sixty-six, and my mother's a teenager again.
Ella glides on stage in a long, orange, spangled gown,
round glasses flashing, and she pours out the gold.
Forget arthritis, forget worn out, forget things to do,
forget supper to cook, forget this battle or that,
forget it. If one of Ella's records starts to play,
Mama's spine sits up and takes notice, her knees bounce,
and her feet start to hop. Ella's singing. Ella's swinging.
Ella's making the living easy. Now, the brightest spangles
are the ones flying out of Ella's throat, charging the air
all the way to the nosebleeds, blowing down the theater walls
behind us, from the first stretched and twisted tones to the last,
showering everything with syncopated stardust.

II

When Ella sings, she dances a stairway of twenty-four notes,
brings a basketful of strawberries, warm bread
and sweet butter, summer heat shimmering,
clouds scudding, chasing blue skies after a storm.

When Ella sings, she spreads her song like a quilt of velvet chords
wrapped around lonely, a dreamwork of sighs,
a belly full of ache, an earthquake in the heart.
She mesmerizes devils, calls forth angels.

When Ella sings, her voice becomes a dream of flying,
darting here and there, hovering, weaving like a web,
like a dragonfly wing, catching each facet of the light,
glistening fractals, tangles, bangles, and beads.

When Ella sings, she pours the clean, clear, cold water
over the stones of living, over and down, sliding,
slipping into a pool below, splashing as it falls.
She wipes her brow, dries our sorry tears.

When Ella sings, she lingers long at that deep, blue pool.
Mist rises. Light refracts. Then her song swims out,
past the breakers, then farther still, to a calm sea, bobs and floats there,
slowly turns, begins to stroke back, gathers strength, swells, rises

on the crest of a wave she herself is shaping, a curving rhythm
she is riding, and she carries us with her, over and over, pulling
the ropes tied at the very core, until finally, the crescendo
before she lays us down, ever so gently, back on the shore.

Singing "Stardust" the Night Before

Everyone's gone to rest, but my head's
lying next to hers on the hospital bed.
The low light from the kitchen shows
her profile, eyes shut, mouth slack.
For now, the slight gurgle is gone.

My right arm's falling asleep, my left hand
placed over the blanket, ready to hold on
if the agony returns. I sing in her ear,
a little off-key, from memory, conjuring
Hoagie's tune that coils up and up and down.

For hours today, she has ridden
a runaway train, strained to escape,
begged NO, crushed everyone's fingers.
My voice falters on *dream in vain*, but
I push through the lump and try to call

love through my throat, to transfuse
a faraway dream through her ear:
her look adoring, dancing with my father,
his arms claiming her, her body cleaving to his.
Oh, my, they could dance.

I want this song to carry her
off this track to another time,
a big band spinning a mixed-up, perfect
melody of now and next and long ago,
notes that dip low, then linger, then yearn.

Her eyebrows begin to lift with the tune,
then she opens her eyes, as I repeat,
again, the last refrain, and she looks up
at the ceiling, and smiles at someone,
coyly tilts her face, and then she lifts her arms

from under the covers, and I watch with wonder
as she raises both arms, wraps them—I see now—
around his neck, pulls herself to him, long ago,
pulls him to her, in the dusk, how she presses
her lips, impossibly, once again, to his.

Five

Forest Salutation

Plant yourself
ankle deep
in a vernal pool
of mayapples

Arch your neck back
and stretch

Sightline
to the greening tips
of poplars
reaching
reaching

Kneel

Lift waxy veils
to reveal
singular blossoms

Adjust your vision
to the flowers

Breathe in
their glowing light

Repeat

Dream of the Homeplace

The oaks regrown, cornfields stretching to woods,
hickory standing, unstruck by lightning.
Slam of the screen door, climb to the attic,
bare feet parting dust like fish part water.
Boxes spill, his pole and rusted tackle,
her wedding dress ghost floats by the window.
A dull slapping sound, wake against a boat,
as a storm picks up, and I periscope
out of the house. Laundry flaps on the line.
Silver slashes of sudden summer rain

stroke their way up the hill, bending the stalks
row by row, and my hair has grown wispy
and wild, lifting, swaying in the currents
like seaweed, petrichor rising, rushing
across the meadow, a benediction.
My long gown wraps me like a winding sheet,
my beard white and thick as Methuselah's,
glinting with bits caught there like shiny lures
in a tangled fisherman's line, dangling,
a seed pod, an old key, a golden charm.

When I wake up, the homeplace is still gone.
The garden is still cemented over.
There is nothing there now but roads and shops,
bleached bone sidewalks, a dense townhouse forest.
No watery breezes through high trees there,

no orioles weaving a teardrop nest,
no fireflies swim in darkening green there,
no drops on the sill now, no dear ones, no door.
Everything is gone now, but the dry
wind of memory, against which I lean.

Dancing in the Dining Room

The way your shoes elbow mine,
the smooth conversation of our hips,
the way my thoughts seem to dangle in air
like paper lanterns in summer—

we turn across the cool wooden floor
and plunge barefoot
into Saturday night's musky freedom
though it's only a Monday.

Time is a too-tight skin we let fall away
while Stevie sings, and we break into smiles
like sun through a rainstorm
and tuck our heads together.

Yes, sometimes past loneliness lingers,
the music's undertow,
a little growl inside the purr.
Not tonight.

Tonight the green hush,
the velvet, sleepy dream
brushes its fingers down my spine.

Let's dance on.
Let's make it be daisies.
Let's wind the sweet chain
around and around and around.

In the Produce Section

The Easter lilies trumpet over the vegetables.
I take your hand, pull you to them,
open the petals, lift the stamen,
and the golden yellow pollen
stains my fingers. "Look," I say,
"see how ready." We smile.
No fear, no sadness, only this:

We eat good food, walk through town,
stop under a cloud of white blossoms.
Finally inside, we spell words
with our clothes. "S is for shy,"
I whisper, as I slip off my stockings.

Outside, purple tulips lift to a white moon.
Your hand tells me, *Here is the center.*
Equal bodies, soft slapping of bellies,
kisses, and kisses like sleep,
and then, sleep—

In the Gynecologist's Office

Recall the lover who grunted and groaned over
the lifeless you beneath him, how he closed

his eyes to your blank face, to your hands' limp
resistance against his shoulders. Your body

braced itself as it might tense in the posture
of nightmares. (Think back to crouching in the backseat

as your father takes the corners too fast.)
Lover of the no-talking, no-laughing rule,

no whipped cream for him. You let him happen, and now
you're here: wearing socks, a bra, and turtleneck,

legs dangling over the table, you wait
for the slide of cold metal and the pressure

of rubber fingers. Today the doctor cuts scraps
away, and mouths of blood open and say, perhaps

you will die. But first, he smears your tissue
on a slide. The soft blue walls are splashed

with stories of surrender. Next, a cone of flesh,
the disappearance of the doorway to your self.

And then, the small fist of endurance
that keeps you in balance. For this,

there should have been whipped cream, ripe figs,
two bodies swimming in sweat. For this,

there should have been a lover's constant
whispering, lips caressing your hair. For this,

a man who rolls you over in his mouth
like a hard word, sounding out your meanings.

Postcard

A surprise from somewhere you've never
been, or maybe remember as a spot
where you stood looking at the scenery.
Or say it's from a friend in New York,
a diner in her working-class neighborhood,
aluminum sided like a giant
sardine can—pink vinyl and chrome edged
Formica tables, specked gray and white.
And suddenly you're sixteen again, tearing
off to the Double T, pretending to be
a grown-up, smoking and drinking coffee
with your best friend in a booth by a window.
You order a Double T burger and fries,
chocolate cream pie. And the waitress
who's worked there twenty years puts her pencil
behind her ear and says, "Is that all, hon?"
like any good Baltimore waitress should.
You laugh at the fat trucker at the counter,
how his butt is sticking out over his jeans,
but you're really staring out the window,
at the rainy traffic on Route 40,
thinking about the boy who always drives
you home. You reel and giggle when he does
donuts in the parking lot, and you yell
for him to stop though you wish you'd never
leave that car. His face still floats up sometimes,
in a dream, a postcard from the past:
you bike along his street and meet once again,

after years, and he asks you in—you discover
it's not the same house, but his smell is still
part sweat, part cotton, part fresh cut wood.
You can't linger there, in that time when
who you are now doesn't count. You're drawn up,
out of the story and back onto the straight line
of your life. You feel yourself rolling through
the routine, energy waxing and waning each day
at the same time. And soon it is next year,
and then the year after. Stacked away in a box,
letters and postcards: you shuffle them, hoping to
draw the card that can bring you back to the you
who lies smoldering under the surface, the one
who keeps secret desires tucked away
in her pockets. What happens when one slips out?
Does it snake its way up your spine?
Does it fill your head once more,
like the scent of an old lover? You want
to get away, to go far enough away
that a strange room feels familiar, safe,
a place to sleep, to think. And before you
come home, you'll write a postcard, a small
surprise for a friend who finds it in the mail,
looks at the front, reads the message and smiles:
"The mornings are peaceful. There's sun
on the mountain and fog down below."

If Our Eyes Were Able,
We Would Find the Sky

...from the reflection of this light the air
all around will be colored as we
see it to be, as the sun shines upon its parts...
—Epicurus of Samos

Even though we both stand on the porch and trace
the double curve over the valley, we don't

see the same rainbows. Waves of light pass through
drops of water and break open along a single line of sight.

Tree swallows swoop over the meadow, and two rabbits
step onto the lawn from the tall grass. The first bow

bends across a plane of air. Then the second appears,
then disappears, now on this side, now on that,

a magician's trick of red to violet, violet
to red, now you see it, now you don't.

The deeper blue between the two is a trap door
holding in the light, which enters but can't return,

Alexander's Dark Band. He explained it first
in the year 200. Imagine taking time to stop

and ponder rain. Some accident of light, the optics
of possibility and limit. Something breaks each of us open

eventually, try as we might. It's not easy
to reveal our own surprising set of parts.

The way a page in a book cracks open the world's colors.
Or the first time I met your face, shining like an old friend

stepping off a train, igniting a thundercloud
in my chest. A double rainbow is gift enough.

Soon the rain and clouds move away to the east.
Centuries later, Felix Billet saw nineteen bows

in his light chamber. *If our eyes were able*, he said,
we would find the sky filled with arcs, arcs crossing

wider arcs, almost into infinity. A rose of rainbows,
he called it. Perhaps when one body passes through

another, it leaves a trail in the sky of memory,
like the shadow of the mountain walking across the valley,

the familiar space which tracks between us,
the swallows on the birdhouse, the rabbits

grazing in tandem. The rainbow is not located
in the sky. It travels in waves to our eyes.

Ephemera

Red dawn on the mountain,
light filtering bare trees,
bloodroot, hepatica, trout lily,
fungal blooms waking the ants,
match flames of spring.

Bees, still drowsy with cold,
taking first sips. Waning moon
crossing a window, a kiss
before sleep. Sleep itself, or
any kiss, or any night,

or the mystic lantern of a dream,
glowing from core to fingertips.
Words blading a page, swirling
mayflies, a feathery whisper,
passing as the heron over

the meadow to the pond,
wingbeats slowing, shifting, lifting,
marking a life. I am saying nothing
as tenderly as I can. A lily opening
on any pond. Any pond, any lily.

A pulse, a pulsar, starlight pouring
millennia at a glance. All this rising
and falling, all this tunneling the anthills
of perception. All of this. Sweet sips
of here, now, look, *this*, yes! Then gone.

The Mayapple Forest

She does not walk in bare feet on damp leaves,
light on spongy ground.
She does not cup a pale green bud,
still and swelling, in her curious palm.

She comes and goes, looks at me
with large brown eyes she doesn't have,
eyes like her father's.
When she does not smile, her dimples show,

like mine. My daughter, Lucy Rose,
the one I do not have.
Lucinda for my great-great-grandmother.
Rose for old fashioned, rambling ones,

yellow as rich cream, simply petaled, and fragrant.
We don't hold hands or turn around the fairy ring
of mushrooms rising in the orchard.
She does not remind me to sit by the stream,

to let my mind move with watery light.
The mayapples rise as the wheel turns,
lifting their shining shoulders. One morning, not there,
the next, dozens of glistening sheaths, pushing up

from the womb of the forest floor, leaves closed
as the stem lengthens, all sprung from one root,

connected, slowly unfolding, opening bright umbrella
selves almost in unison, waxy and wrinkled,

discovering their shape, then flexing out fully,
tip to tip, a green quilt of six-pointed stars at my feet.
Lucy Rose doesn't know why she's drawn here,
when she doesn't come walking.

She does not ask me to lie down here,
on the reassuring earth, though I do as she says.
Be very still. Be an acorn falling.
Here, underneath, look up—

Breathe in the singular flowers
nodding from the axil of two leaves
on the female stems, pale chiffon faces
across the colony, turned each to each.

One or two facing slightly away,
lost in thought, circle of children
gathering to play under a bright moon,
pale stones set just so in a shaded garden.

I do not see her moving beneath this tender sky
inches above the litterfall.
I do not see her, as she touches a stalk here
or there, or as she reaches to finger the first pale fruit.

She is not listening to the oak and its saplings.
She does not call me to join her. She leaves
no shadow. She doesn't turn back.
Farther and farther into the dappled tangle

until she might be just a leaf
rustling under the mayapple forest.
The world accepts its own dying,
recreates itself, cell by cell.

May the Particles of My Body
Travel the Endless Conduits

My father came to me in a dream
a week after he died, knocked on the front
door and grinned in the summer night air.
He glowed from some unseen, amber neon.
Everything is fine, he said. *I wanted
you to know.* Then a beam of light, bright
and cool, just took him, carried him down
the road like high beams sliding a bedroom wall,
a shadow's opposite.

                    Home in dreams
is the house on the hill, trouble is the Sunday school.
Tonight, the moon taps me on the shoulder,
floating in an unmoored boat, my mind rocked
awake. I used to argue with the teacher.
His name was Vernon, which means "alder grove."
He insisted God was an old, bearded white man
on a cloud, I swear to you, and we were made
in his image. He's buried just feet from our family stones.

When I die, lay me in the loam under the big oak
on the path through the woods, deep down in the endless
flow of talk among the trees there, from the centurion
to the saplings. Sometimes I sense it passing under
my feet there, like a bird overhead on a bright day,
but in reverse. May the particles of my body
travel the endless conduits.

I wish I had the right words
to part the sea of all the nonsense and save us all
from drowning. Quiet those commandments.
Press my ear to earth and listen hard.
A network of souls whispers, and the dark matter stretches,
an infinite stream we swim and swim.
That's one image from which we're made, Vernon.
The alder grove's another. Try to remember
what cannot nor ever will be named.
All that we are is this river of light.

Acknowledgments

Thank you to the editors of the following publications in which these poems first appeared, sometimes in earlier forms:

Artemis: "I Want to Ride Through this Life"

Autumn Sky Poetry Daily: "Life Goals"

Banyan Review: "Cicatrice"

The Blue Nib: "Cool Glass of Water," "Death in Spring," "Golden Purslane," *"Hope is the Thing with Feathers"*

Blueline: "Summer Storms"

Cider Press Review: "Love, Birds"

december: "May the Particles of My Body Travel the Endless Conduits"

Galway Review: "Barn Owl," "Please Forgive Me," "Upstream"

Lothlorien Poetry Journal: "Concerning Stars," "Dream of the Homeplace," "Forest Salutation," "If Our Eyes Were Able"

Poetry Ireland Review: "The Mayapple Forest"

Prairie Schooner: "Dancing in the Dining Room," "The Taste of Copper"

Redheaded Stepchild: "The Daily Subtraction of Grief"

One Tree Many Branches: "I Watch My Sister Harvest Lavender"

Rocky Mountain Review: "Postcard"

SWIMM Every Day: "Mayapple Jelly"

In Gratitude

To the poets who taught and mentored me when I was a student—Stephen Behrendt, Michael Collier, Greg Kuzma, Stanley Plumly, Hilda Raz, Marcia Southwick, and Elizabeth Spires—thank you for the strong, long-lived seeds you planted.

To Diane Lockward, thank you for opening the door and ushering this book into the world.

To those who helped me shape and refine the manuscript draft, heartfelt gratitude: Barbara Frye, and fellow members of the Virginia Women's Poetry Collective, April Asbury, Angie Clevenger, Angela Dribben, and Cathy Hailey.

To Sandy Yannone, thank you for the poetic collaboration, inspiration, and Cultivating Voices LIVE Poetry.

To Terry Whye and Kelley Gordon, thank you for your steadfast encouragement, my sisters.

To Judy James, thank you for cheering me on.

To Doug Parsons, for your love and belief in me.

About the Author

Kim Ports Parsons grew up in the countryside near Baltimore and earned degrees from Goucher College, University of Maryland, and University of Nebraska-Lincoln. She taught students of all ages for decades, and worked in public and school libraries. Her poems have been published in many journals and anthologies. Kim volunteers weekly for Cultivating Voices LIVE Poetry, an international, intersectional, intergenerational poetry community. She lives next to Shenandoah National Park, gardens, walks, and writes. *The Mayapple Forest* is her debut collection.

www.KimPortsParsons.com

CPSIA information can be obtained
at www.ICGtesting.com
Printed in the USA
LVHW110048111022
730380LV00004B/247